Big
Weather

Zoë Clarke

Illustrated by **Venitia Dean**

OXFORD
UNIVERSITY PRESS

Contents

Extreme Weather

Take a look out of your window – is it sunny, snowy, rainy or windy? Is it time to grab your sunglasses, or to throw on a jumper? If there is lightning flashing, or if loads of hailstones are bouncing on the ground, you might want to stay inside!

Sometimes the winds are stronger and wilder than normal, the amount of snow or ice is heavier, or storms of sand and dust fill the sky. Weather like this does not happen every day, but when it does, you know you have got *BIG* weather!

The Big Freeze

Snow is great!
You can build snowmen and
go sledging. But snow can cause big problems.
In some parts of the United States of America
(USA), 16 metres of snow can fall in the winter.
Extreme snow can be so deep it can bury a house.

Beware of the blizzard!

A huge 30 centimetres of snow fell overnight in New York, USA. There were also strong winds which created a blizzard.

Take care out there! Blizzards last for over three hours and make it very difficult to see.

Where is my car?

The wind has pushed the snow into deep piles called drifts.

Ice storms

Snowstorms can turn into something even more dangerous ... ice storms.
Ice might look like icing on a cake, but an ice storm can split trees, snap
telephone poles and bend metal **pylons** in half.

Look at what a few centimetres of ice can do!

In Toronto, Canada, one of
the worst ice storms snapped
power lines and left thousands
of people without electricity
in December 2013.

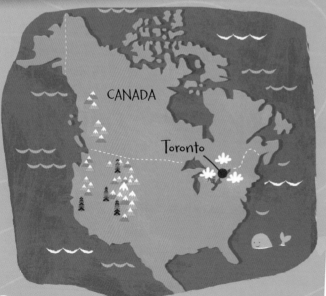

What turns a snowstorm into an ice storm?

When snow turns into freezing rain and hits cold surfaces, it turns to ice in seconds. This ice can be up to five centimetres thick.

Temperatures below freezing

Drops of water freeze into snowflakes high in the atmosphere.

Temperatures above freezing

The snowflakes turn into rain when they pass through warm air.

Temperatures below freezing

When the temperature is very low near the ground, the rain turns into freezing rain.

Freezing rain hits cold surfaces and turns into ice.

Ice shoves

wind + ice + water = trouble

When ocean **currents** or strong winds force big chunks of ice across a sea or lake, you get an ice shove. The ice is crushed together and it piles up into massive walls, reaching up to 12 metres high. That's taller than two double-decker buses on top of each other!

The ice doesn't stop when it reaches the shore; it keeps moving slowly forwards, piling up higher and higher. The frozen waves of an ice shove can destroy everything in their path, and even swallow houses.

Ice shove fact file

An ice shove is also called an ice **tsunami**.

An ice shove on the shore of Lake Winnebago, USA in 2013.

The ice shove kept moving, and smashed through doors and windows of houses.

Spinning Storms

In the USA alone, over 1000 tornadoes are reported every year. Check out this deadly windy weather.

Tornadoes are also called 'twisters'.

How to make a tornado!

1 Start a thunderstorm

Thunderclouds form when warm air rises into the sky and cools into a cloud.

2 Grow your thundercloud

The thundercloud grows. More warm air is sucked up.

4 Vortex

The **vortex** of air spins faster and faster into a tornado.

3 Spin it!

Winds under the thundercloud make the rising air spin.

In 2013, one deadly tornado in Oklahoma, USA destroyed over 1000 buildings and killed 25 people. It had a wind speed of up to 321 kilometres per hour. Some tornadoes can pick up things like trucks and carry them away.

Hurricanes, typhoons and tropical cyclones

Q: What's the difference between a hurricane, a typhoon and a tropical cyclone?

A: Nothing. They are all spinning storms, they all start over water and they all have wind speeds of over 119 kilometres per hour. They have different names because they happen in different parts of the world.

*A spinning storm photographed from space. You can see the **eye of the storm**.*

Ocean	Spinning storm name
Atlantic and north-east Pacific	hurricane
North-west Pacific	typhoon
South Pacific and Indian	cyclone or tropical cyclone

How to make a tropical storm

2 Ocean winds make the rising air spin.

3 High in the sky, the air cools and falls back down.

1 Strong winds pull moisture from the ocean into the sky, where it forms clouds.

4 Giant cycles of air keep feeding the storm.

Spinning storm statistics

The circling winds of a hurricane, typhoon or tropical cyclone can reach over 14 kilometres high, 1500 kilometres wide, and move as fast as 300 kilometres per hour. When these winds reach land, they can cause tremendous damage.

When is a typhoon a super typhoon?

When the word 'super' is used to describe a storm, it means that the storm is bigger and stronger than any other.

Typhoon Haiyan fact file

In 2013, Typhoon Haiyan started over the Pacific Ocean. It moved towards the Philippines but instead of dying out over the water like many typhoons, it became a super typhoon and reached land.

Typhoon Haiyan's deadly path

region of heaviest impact

Winds of up to 240 kilometres per hour sent waves of water over the islands and swallowed towns and villages. Over 14 million people were affected by the typhoon, and over 6000 people died.

This is how Typhoon Haiyan looked from space. Can you see the eye of the storm?

Super Typhoon Haiyan threw these huge ships out of the water.

Dry Storms

You don't always need rain, snow or hail to make a storm. Sometimes big weather starts on the ground.

⚠ Dust and sand

In very dry places, like deserts, strong winds can blow fine dust up to seven kilometres into the air. This fine powder turns into a dust fog and is blown thousands of kilometers away.

You can't hear these dry storms approaching. But when you see a wall of dust or sand coming towards you, be prepared for the sky to go dark, sometimes for days. From May to September there can be dry storms every day in countries where there are deserts.

Sandstorm fact file

Sandstorms in the Sahara Desert can be so big, they would cover an area the size of Britain!

Fire tornadoes

Think of a spinning storm made of fire, and you have a fire tornado. But the fire does not start from the sky, and it's not attached to a cloud. Incredibly, it starts on the ground as a wildfire and *rises* into the sky.

3 Winds make the hot air and the flames spin.

The flames grow and the air heats up. The hot air rises.

2

1 A wildfire starts in areas such as forests or grasslands. The fire burns on the ground.

4 The fire dries out the wood around it. More trees burn and make the fire bigger. The wind adds more air to the flames, making them stronger.

⚠ Fire tornado fact file

Fire tornadoes can be 10–50 metres wide, but they usually only last a few minutes.

Space Storms

Not all storms happen on Earth – there is big weather in space too.

Solar flare

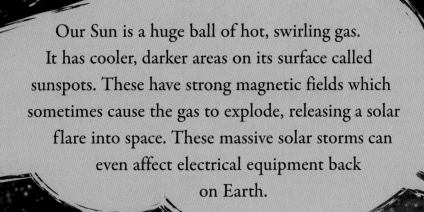

Our Sun is a huge ball of hot, swirling gas. It has cooler, darker areas on its surface called sunspots. These have strong magnetic fields which sometimes cause the gas to explode, releasing a solar flare into space. These massive solar storms can even affect electrical equipment back on Earth.

Planets have big weather too; **satellites** have spotted hurricanes on Saturn and giant dust storms on Mars. Amazingly, there is one space storm that is so big you can see it from Earth, using a telescope. The storm is called the Great Red Spot, and it is on the planet Jupiter. The storm was first seen in the 17th century, which means it has been continuing for over 300 years.

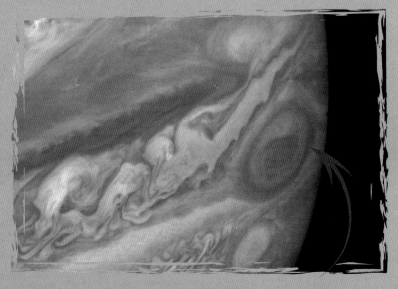

Great Red Spot on Jupiter

Storm Trackers

Weather experts can warn people if dangerous weather is on the way, thanks to some amazing technology.

Weather satellites

Weather satellites like this one float over 35 000 kilometres above Earth.

Q: How does a satellite track big weather?

A: The satellite has a digital camera which takes pictures from space. These pictures are sent back to a control centre on Earth. The satellite also has **sensors** which record how hot or cold the weather is.

Weather forecasters study all this infomation to predict what the weather will be doing *before* it actually happens. This information becomes a weather forecast.

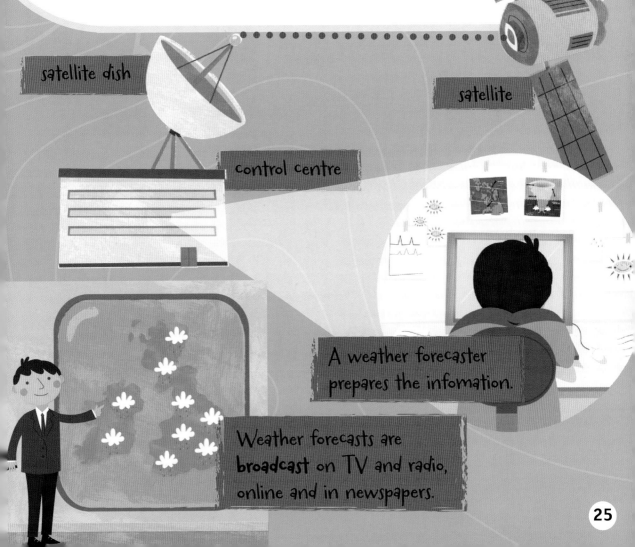

satellite dish

satellite

control centre

A weather forecaster prepares the infomation.

Weather forecasts are broadcast on TV and radio, online and in newspapers.

Staying Safe

⚠ BE ALERT!

When extreme weather is on the way, listen to the local news and weather forecasts, which will tell you how to stay safe.

But what if you do not have a TV or radio? In Bangladesh, **volunteers** on bicycles and motorcycles ride through the streets and use **megaphones** to warn people about storms.

🚫 DON'T PANIC!

These special planes carry water in tanks. The water is used to put out wildfires and fire tornadoes.

HELP IS ON THE WAY!

Roads can be cleared quickly after heavy snow with snow blowers, which suck up the snow like a vacuum cleaner and blow it away.

Snow Canyon, Japan, open to traffic!

Big Weather, Big Problem?

We've learned that extreme weather can do big damage, but big weather can be helpful too.

Hurricanes can sometimes build up areas of sand called 'barrier islands', which protect the main coast from being battered by the sea.

A barrier island off the east coast of the USA.

During a hurricane, these islands can get higher and wider because sand is blown there by the wind. Without this extra sand, some of the islands might disappear.

Weather-proofing the future

No need to panic – experts are getting better at understanding big weather. This means that people are able to protect themselves and their homes.

This floating building design might be the answer for people living in areas where there's lots of flooding.

Buildings can be built to survive – whatever the weather. Just remember to check the forecast before you go out today!

Glossary

broadcast: send infomation as a radio or TV programme

currents: movements of water

eye of the storm: a calm area at the centre of a storm

megaphones: cone-shaped devices to make sounds louder

pylons: structures that support power lines

satellites: electronic objects orbiting planets

sensors: devices that receive and send information

tornadoes: powerful and destructive spinning columns of air

tsunami: a series of water waves caused by a landslide, volcanic eruption or earthquake

volunteers: people who offer to do something

vortex: a rotating mass of air

Index

About the Author

I've been stuck in the snow, drenched by rain, hit by hailstones and battered by the wind. I've never got close to a fire tornado, or battled against a hurricane, or been blinded in a dust storm, but when I was researching this book, I read lots of stories about the courage and bravery of people who have survived big weather.

Greg Foot, Series Editor

I've loved science ever since the day I took my papier mâché volcano into school. I filled it with far too much baking powder, vinegar and red food colouring, and WHOOSH! I covered the classroom ceiling in red goo. Now I've got the best job in the world: I present TV shows for the BBC, answer kids' science questions on YouTube, and make huge explosions on stage at festivals!

Working on TreeTops inFact has been great fun. There are so many brilliant books, and guess what ... they're all packed full of awesome facts! What's your favourite?